cramoisie

Danya Wadi

BookLeaf Publishing

India | USA | UK

Presentation by *BookLeaf Publishing*

Web: www.bookleafpub.com

E-mail: info@bookleafpub.com

ISBN: 9789360949419

First edition 2024

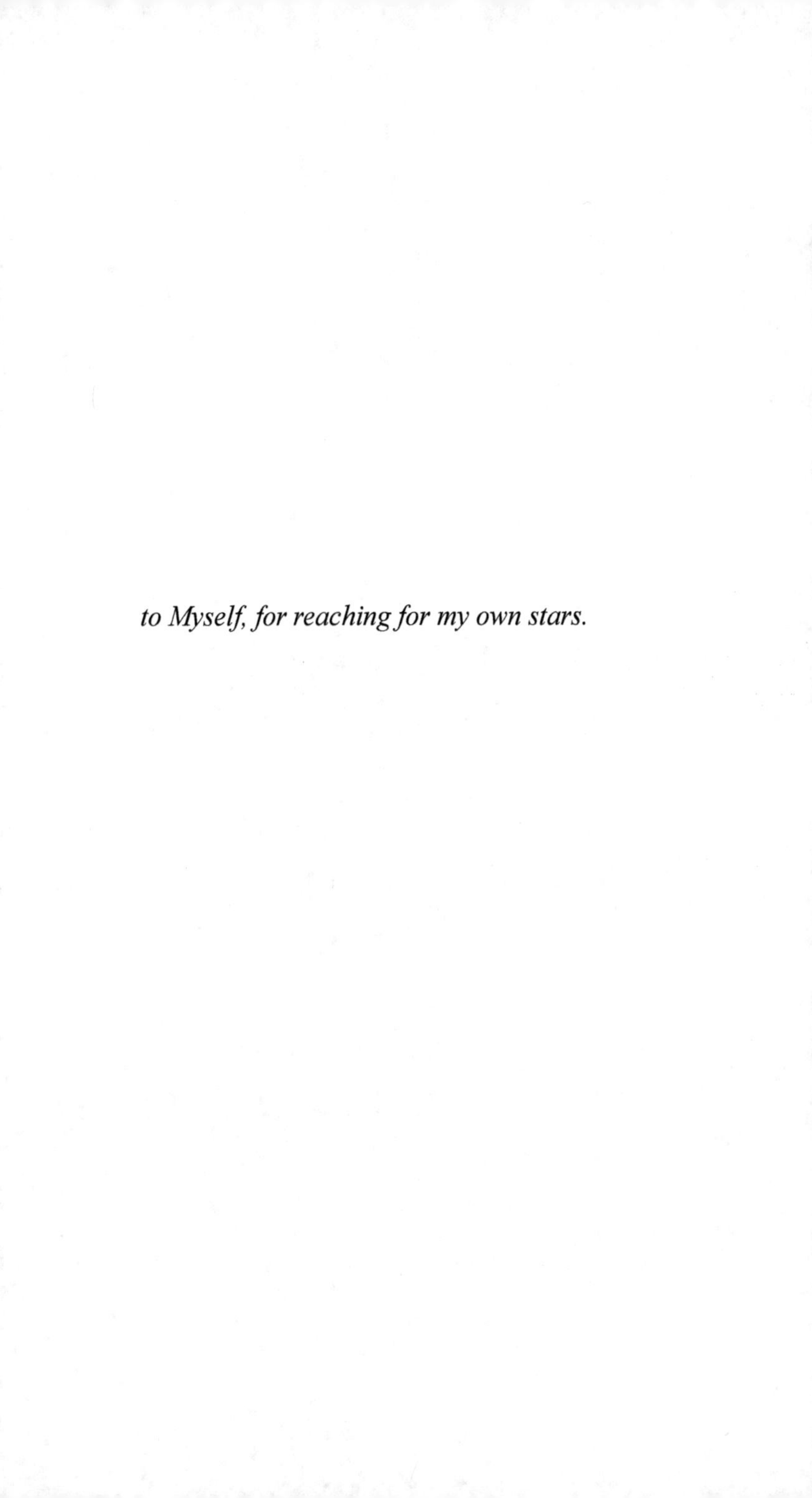

to Myself, for reaching for my own stars.

lovely words

i was nothing to you,
right?
the way you would yell,
convince me of things i hadn't said,
i was nothing to you,
i meant no more than the earth beneath your
boots,
you used me as a keepsake,
a treasure trove of all of your insecurities,
any and all guilt you were capable of.

and i kept it as my own,
just so,
it wouldn't burden you,
how could i in good conscious,
place more strain on your already breaking
back?
a back that was breaking for me,
because of me.

you lived to show me your adoration,
with all your sugary names for me,
and i,
i lived for those words uttered from you,
they made me cry,

they made me ache,
they made me wail,
in ways,
i was not aware a human could.

but that was just how i showed you my love,
and once you saw,
how tightly i grasped on to you,
after you gashed me with your affection,
you only gave me more,
and more,
and more.

until you were so incredulously sweet,
and i,
i realized,
my frail hands- clasped around my three rotten
teeth.

l.w.h

thank you,
thank you ever so much darling,
for a freedom you have given me,
that i couldn't give myself,
thank you my sweet love,
for the pain working its way through my limbs,
teaching me that some things will only end,

without you,
future disappointments,
would have been,
too much to bear,
so thank you for stepping on me,
and making me accustomed,
to the silence i must keep,
thank you sweetheart,
for treading on my soul,
thank you,
for teaching me not to give away,
too much of myself,
not to feel too deep,
thank you honey,
thank you oh so much,
for killing me when i couldn't.

poachers pride

do you despise me?
everytime you look at me do you taste dirt in
your mouth?
do you fill yourself with contempt at the
mention of my name?
or have you numbed yourself to the nuisance,
because,
 to you I am nothing more than an animal,
and you've turned yourself into the poacher.

his

never was there a time before i felt this way,
for countless years,
he was the light of my life,
when i really heard his voice,
i was tearfully happy for the first time,

i don't know what happened inside me,
i had once held us so closely together,
and now he did,
i needed valleys between us,
he needed to be suffocated more than ever,
it's normal i would tell myself,
and i found myself saying "okay, i love you
too,"
but i felt my bones crumble beneath the weight
of such burdensome lies,
and i longed for nothing more to scream,
i hate you,
"i'm not comfortable" he said,
and sighed so softly,
 i almost mistook it as a sign of sadness.

a curse

why am I stuck in this awful spiral of falling for
dangerous things,
i only seem to love the worst people i've met,
only seeing the beauty in the things i know will
kill me,
i only love the ones that will rip my heart into
pieces,
inevitably,
leaving me looking for another to put the pieces
back together,
but i know,
they will only do the same.

an end, a beginning

it used to feel like home,
my place in your arms,
now it's just become a tinge of unease,
although the dying hydrangeas still remind me
of the color of your eyes,
and the burning diesel in the air still reminds me
of those reckless machines you loved,
your fear of death,
and my invitation to him,
we had the kind of love people wrote songs
about,
we had the kind of love that would inspire artists
to create their masterpieces,
we too created a piece of art,
and god was it to die for.

the first of many

i thought about telling him how badly he had
hurt me,
tortured my poor soul,
with his betrayal,
but there was none,
no commitment between us,
quiet and cacophonous moments,
always holding an aura of peace,
of serenity,
a longing,
maybe,
nothing else was real,
but you could smell the desperation between us
in the air,
the heated first-time touches and messy kisses,
misunderstood tears and aching souls,
and the throbbing,
of knowing i was falling madly in love,
and the throbbing of knowing,
that it was onto the sharpest knife i had ever
seen,
and the throbbing,
of knowing i could do nothing but watch the
blood slowly pour out of me,
but he made that blood flow with such grace,

i almost didn't want it to stop,
my whole life i was yearning to bleed,
and what a better way than he?

and yet i love him

your skin,
the softest velvet,

your voice,
a cascading velvet,

your hands,
a rich velvet,

your skin,
a velvet i thought,
coming to realize briars,

your voice,
a velvet i thought,
coming to realize granite,

your hands,
a velvet i thought,
coming to realize a grip.

a flaw

people measure worth by material,
the more gifts you recieve,
the more worthy of you they seem to become,
how can you judge by currency,
but not,
the bruises left on my arms and heart,
how can you judge what is well for me,
when i myself am nothing to you.

my love, my love, my love

the world feels like its splitting in two,
the trees are shaking their angry fists at me,
at all of us i think,
the sky stays dull and gray,
seems like its always crying these days,
the wind is cold and furious,
its biting at each piece of shared skin,
on days like these there is no separation,
in the from the world,
we feel the same way,
always on the brink of a terrible storm,
on days like these i just turn into another,
i turn into just another,
on days like these when,
my head is a little bit more broken than most,
and even in the face of company i find myself
alone,
i tend to wander outside,
to see the other parts of me,
the things ive become,
as if my innards have somehow been transported
out of me,
reflected in a giant mirror for the rest of the
world to see,
on days like this,

i disappear,
disappear into the rose bushes and under the
willow leaves,
i shy away from the things that walk and talk
and complain and disappoint,
and i find myself telling the sunflowers pretty
stories of us,
and once ive run out of lies,
i tell them the truth of us,
how we were always so close but so far,
and how now my head is always just a little bit
more broken than it used to be,
i just want to disappear on days like these,
when all i can do is conjure up images of us,
if id wished for anything more in my life,

i just wished to be one of the oh so lucky clovers
to be crushed under your boots.

self fulfilling prophecies

you will leave me just as you did her,
you will leave me just as i did him,
you will leave me,
i will beg you to stay,
just as she did,
i will cry and clutch your clothes every night,
before crying myself to sleep,
some nights,
i will lie awake until,
3, 6, 8 a.m,
i will do nothing but think of you,
i will think of your hands,
and how you always placed them tenderly
around my neck,
i will be devastated,
you will leave me,
and you will sever the only thread of hope i ever
had,
you will leave me,
even though you promised so many times,
i was yours forever,
just like you did with her,
you will leave me,
and i will beg you,
"please dont leave me."

but you hold those you love in your hands

i always seemed to be in your hands but not in
your heart,

no,

you never had a heart,

only an illusion of such a blessing to you,

you have soft but callous hands,

you have deep icy eyes that grip those around
you,

you and you,

are two different entities,

there is a you i knew,

and a you i have come to know,

the former the angel,

but the latter always lurks,

the devil always returns,

no matter the lies you powder on top.

does destruction often smell like love?

you have induced an inferno into me,
your distance causing it to eat me inside out,
you try to hang me from the gallows,
"to save me",
but nothing can burn out such insatiable flames,
nothing but more heat,
your gouging fire,
and how impossibly ludicrous it is,
for two infernos to disperse each other,
but theres no other tangible remedy,
the only salvation,
to douse more gasoline unto each other,
so it shall come from eating us,
to driving us,
towards one another,
to bring peace to each others bones,
we must sacrifice ourselves,
creating a new burning,
so it shall come from eating us,
to feeding us.

diffidence

you write about sadness as if you know who she
is,
you act as if she is a constant member of your
life,
although she only comes in fleeting moments
like a mistress
do you even know her?
who is she?
what is she to you?

you write about love as if you know who he is,
you act as if he is a constant member of your
life,
although he only comes in fleeting moments like
a mistress,
do you even know him?
who is he?
what is he to you?

they all do.

my heart resonates with the beauty in swollen
faces and sunken eyes,
with chapped lips and countless bruises,
it resonates with the pale and shaky limbs,
with bitten fingernails and an ugly reality,
my heart resonates with all the things,
 you always found so repulsive,
with every single thing that wont ever,
remind me of you.

a small death

even as i spoke the words they felt wrong,
before they bounded off the tip of my tongue,
the truth of lies was reverberating through each
of them,
cracking voices held memories of old stained
tears,
and hollows blossoming in my chest,
the weight of their absolute falseness crushing
my bones,
i ache for it to be the truth,
but i feel their wrongness,
they taste so bitter.

why?

nobody ever prepares you,
for moments like this,
they tell you all about addictions,
smoking will kill you,
drinking will kill you,
amphetamines,
cocaine,
acid,
will kill you,
but they never warn you,
about him.

the men closest to a contained fire

there an insatiable fire in you,
every time you try to put out your flames,
you only douse it in gasoline,
many would describe you as a house fire,
but i dont think so,
you weren't made to burn old memories,
leaving old empty ash behind,
you were a forest fire,
destroying anything that came close,
you dont leave charred supports,
you leave the stench of death behind you.

duality

you never loved me on those days,
when i would lie silent and you screaming,
you only loved me when i was complacent and
objectified,
never when i refused to give up my mind,
you only loved me when i was too drained to
fight,
i knew,
but i would always make excuses for you,
i knew you could never love who i was,
you only loved me for what you thought i would
become,
and i hope your heart is aching,
i hope it aches for all those moments you held
me,
i hope it aches for all those times you would yell
and call me worthless,
i hope one day you realize that you never loved
me,

and that was your biggest mistake.

it always is

often times
i will think i shouldve let you pass me by
never known the ecstasy of your fingers on my
throat
never undergone the high of your grip on my
hips
never witnessed the beauty of your teeth on my
skin
never screamed under your tongue and lips
often times
i will think i shouldve let you pass me by
because as things come together
they always come undone
no matter how much i wish
your ropes cannot hold me forever
and neither can those enticing eyes
fates hold a tighter bind than yours
often times
i ask
if the love will be worth the pain
I speak to the blank air
for not even i can stop either
only able to sigh
as your blades kiss my skin
often times

i think
"i hope this isn't the last time"

i never succeed

some days,
i may succeed,
in occupying my brain just enough,
just enough,
to keep your memories away,
just enough,
to keep myself from remembering your touch,
most days,
i may succeed,
in occupying my brain just enough,
just enough,
to never linger on your smell,
just enough,
to keep you out,
those days,
where i wont succeed,
in occupying my brain just enough,
just enough,
not to remember how you taste,
just enough,
not to feel you choking me.